# Are We the Same?

### Ancillary Book for Parents, Teachers and SLOs

*An easy-to-follow guide for all facilitators, parents, foster families, caregivers, teachers & School Learning Support Officers (SLSOs)*

## ITHIA FARAH

DoctorZed
Publishing
www.doctorzed.com

This edition published 2020 by DoctorZed Publishing.
10 Vista Ave, Skye, South Australia 5072
www.doctorzed.com
orders@doctorzed.com

ISBN: 978-0-6488271-5-3 (hc)
ISBN: 978-0-6488271-4-6 (sc)
ISBN: 978-0-6488271-3-9 (e)

A CiP number can be found at the National Library of Australia.

First edition published by Memnon Edições Científicas Ltda 1998, 1999, 2006, 2018, 2019.
www.memnon.com.br

Because of the dynamic nature of the Internet, any web addresses or links in this book may have changed since publication and may no longer be valid. The views expressed in this work are solely those of the author and do not necessarily reflect the views of the publisher and the publisher hereby disclaims any responsibility for them.

The author of this book does not dispense medical advice or prescribe the use of any technique as a form of treatment for physical, emotional, or medical diagnoses without the advice of a physician, either directly or indirectly. The intent of the author is only to offer information of a general nature to help you in your quest for emotional health and wellbeing. In the event you use any of the information in this book for yourself, which is your constitutional right, the author and the publisher assume no responsibility for your actions.

Any people depicted in stock imagery are models and such images are being used for illustrative purposes only.

Cover imagery © Ithia Farah

Printed in the United States of America, Australia & UK.

DoctorZed Publishing rev. date: 08/08/2020

# Contents

# Acknowledgements

*This work represents the efforts and commitment of many people that contributed to this book:*

*To those who inspired me along my professional journey,*

*I want to extend a special thank you to all my clinical supervisors; my mentors; my colleagues; my family and my brother Eduardo Farah for his amazing support.*

*Most of all, thank you for my clients: children and their families, all caregivers or parents whose dedication is genuinely inspiring and continue to teach me so much about how to be a better professional every day, in Brazil and Australia.*

*Thank you for your trust and for allowing me to serve you!*

*Ithia Farah*

*"How wonderful it is that nobody need wait a single moment before starting to improve the world."*

Anne Frank

# The Power to Change

*"The possibility of a truly just and free society begins with how we see and nurture our children.""*
– Professor Stuart Shanker

We have an incredible power to change ourselves and inspire change in other people's lives. It is essential to be aware of the responsibility that comes with this power so that we use it wisely, particularly with reference to families and children receiving our support and guidance. Children have 'sponge-like' minds that absorb information very easily. They are influenced by our attitudes, our world-view, our prejudices, and our beliefs. We can unintentionally pass on our views to those around us, through verbal or nonverbal signs, words and actions, and even our silence. Inclusion is the deliberate act of welcoming diversity, respecting differences, and creating a safe environment where all kinds of people can thrive and succeed in a community that recognises everyone is intrinsically valuable. We all have a role in upholding the strong values and having the tough conversations that build inclusion.

The context of inclusivity is broad. For example, it could relate to income, gender fluidity, disabilities, nationality, religion, food preferences and other choices. So how do we change our mindset and our attitude towards our community? The first step is to recognise that an inclusive society is everyone's responsibility. It's our choice to be active and hands-on in the process.

The *Are We The Same?* ancillary booklet has been written to support teachers, therapists, parents, caregivers and any adults who develop activities with children. This booklet aims to help facilitators to look after themselves and have self-awareness about their feelings and bias. It hopes to inspire adults to have that 'awkward conversation' with children, to not to be frightened to talk, to understand their reactions and emotions and explore their beliefs together. Respecting that others may have different ideas and make different choices can be a challenge. However, with empathy and kindness, it is possible that we can discover new ways to interact and behave in our society.

## A future with kindness and solidarity

There is still a long way before we achieve a fully inclusive society. Reaching that point is a process. If we are self-aware and build emotional literacy in ourselves first by being good role models, and if we respect other's differences and choices while treating everyone with kindness, children are likely to follow our example.

Taking on this facilitator role goes far beyond delivering the *Are We the Same?* colouring book! It is achieved through reviewing our biases and opening a safe space to discuss feelings. Encouraging children to think and talk is a process of capacity building which supports children to learn how to make informed choices and have a proactive attitude towards the world. It can be an empowering experience that creates a virtuous and positive circle, where we all grow and become better human beings in a society that respects differences and where we learn from each other.

I believe that YOU can do it! And you?

# About the Project

 *Are We The Same?* is an evidence-based practice activity book with scientifically based guidelines and strategies to successfully support inclusion in the community and develop social skills with an empirical base. It is an approach for fostering the development of children and is appropriate for use in playgroups, kindergartens, preschool centres and primary schools.

This children's colouring book is the result of a program developed by Clinical Psychologist, Ithia Farah, after three years of research and two years working with 60 children – children with typical development and children with disabilities, children with developmental delay, ADHD, Autism, and other diagnoses, aged 3-12 years old in therapeutic group settings in a day-care centre in São Paulo, Brazil.

In the beginning, the book was one of several strategies used to support the inclusion of children with disabilities in regular childcare centres and schools. In 1999, after one year, the project expanded to promote activities that would support children's self-awareness through understanding feelings and behaviours, as well as provide support to parents, caregivers and teachers to build on these strategies, at home or at school.

*Are We The Same?* aims to foster and facilitate the process of respecting diversity, learning about emotional literacy, and identifying, understanding, and responding to emotions - in oneself and others - in a healthy manner.

The program teaches perspective-taking skills that enable children to gain insight, reflect and give their opinions, to think about how they feel physically and emotionally and to think about how others feel and seek solutions. This promotes empathy and mutual respect. Children are encouraged to be aware of how emotions are reflected in their bodies and how to develop a sense of social responsibility towards one other.

The *Are We The Same?* ancillary book resource is an optional addition, with easy to follow steps and suggestions, to accompany the children's book. It is aimed to promote creative ideas that can be used by therapists, SLSOs and clinicians, or in groups of parents/teachers as parallel workshops, in classrooms and family settings.

The age range suggested for this book is 3-10 years old, but may extend to secondary school level, depending on a child's development.

**Are We The Same? has two parts:**

- *Are We The Same?* ancillary booklet: tutorials and suggestions for all facilitators on how to best use the activities, with a description of each strategy and how to apply it with the children during the play group. This dynamic process has better results if family and children engage in the activities on a weekly basis.

- *Are We The Same?* colouring activity book for children.

**Goals:**

There were five main goals for the *Are We the Same?* project:

1. Develop an evidence-based visual resource to improve children's comprehension and learning and promote capacity building for parents, caregivers and teachers, through exploring strategies to best support all children and their families.

2. Promote a strengths-based approach and actively encourage children to have self-awareness and empathy, by identifying and building on their strengths.

3. Create a collaborative learning environment that supports a person-centred approach, encouraging feedback playfully and inter-actively, to develop a positive, ability-focused environment.

4. Design interactive strategies for children to make decisions with unique characters and active participation in the book. Children can familiarise themselves with new concepts, such as abilities and disabilities, and develop a creative thinking process about inclusion as an experience that is part of our daily lives.

5. Promote opportunities to learn skills for life, such as working collaboratively with peers, developing empathy and critical thinking, problem solving skills, improving communication, building self-care, self-regulation, resilience, and self-competence ('I can handle this'). These skills help children learn and are key to their success in school and beyond.

*"High-quality relationships are fundamental to children's resilience. You can develop children's resilience by helping them build and strengthen supportive relationships with their parents and others, and by working with parents and the community to do the same."* Blue, B. Building resilience in children aged 0–12, A practice guide. (2019)

## Communication Skills

Each child develops their communication and speech in a particular way. Sometimes, it is not easy for a child to understand the meaning of an adult's words or gestures, and vice-versa. These challenges with communication difficulties can lead to stress behaviours or challenging behaviours (Shanker, S. 2018). When a child does not know how to communicate what they want (words, gestures, sounds, body language), it is our job to support them and create alternative methods of communication to encourage them to express themselves. When words are not enough, it is time to be creative.

When researching and developing the *Are We The Same?* project, it became apparent that there was a need for visuals support that could promote communication between the clinician and the children, such as drawings of figures as visual aids, to help to make a point or enhance the children's comprehension. The characters were created on the basis of the children's needs: to promote mutual communication, engage participants and help them to retain information.

As much as possible, this booklet encourages the facilitators to use all sensory resources to work with children - "VAK" (Fleming, N. 1987) stands for visual (images), auditory (music, audio and video) and kinaesthetic (group dynamics, exercises, physical work, and a hands-on approach). Using a variety of methods to convey information helps parents and teachers communicate better with children, and helps children communicate better with others (Walsh, B. E. 2011).

### Creative thinking

Children's characters were created during a therapeutic playgroup, in moments of discussion on the topic of the day. Children were expressing various opinions, but because most of them were not yet able to write or read, they seemed confused or distracted by internal or other external stimuli. The way to focus their attention was to eliminate distractions, as much as possible, and to draw some figures that represented their various opinions. This visual aid enhanced and promoted understanding, and it was noticeable that their attention span was significantly improved. The children seemed more interested, looking at the drawings. They began actively participating in discussions and it was a step towards inclusion. The children were able to identify with the characters that the illustrations depicted, so this resource was a great breakthrough for all of us!

Initially, after discussion, the children were given a sheet matrix featuring drawings of children with expressions corresponding to the emotions under discussion (sad, happy, angry, and so on). All the characters we created were given fictitious names and different physical features. The children were asked to talk about their feelings and emotions; afterwards, they added their own drawings to the sheet.

The idea was to support children to share their own emotions; to explain how these emotions were experienced in their bodies, and to show how they expressed these emotions in different situations with their peers.

The children were very receptive and associated the characters with people they knew, "This one looks like..."

The therapeutic play group provided the content to author the book, and to develop the illustrations as the subjects were emerging, with scenes and facts observed during the daily interactions. Two creative children, Emily and Kim, both with physical disabilities, made a precious contribution: reviewed content, shared suggestions, and approved the central themes of the book.

Educating families of typically developing children around how to engage with their peers, learn about respect, tolerance and empathy has shifted these children's perceptions and their families, enabled them to have more positive interactions and allowed them to view their peers in a new social light.

 **A systemic, participative, and interactive process**

The *Are We The Same?* ancillary book enables facilitators to use the suggested strategies to support children in building social skills, learning new perceptions and behaviours, and promoting opportunities to develop core concepts involved in Theory of Mind (Kloo et al., 2010)

The various themes can be addressed and explored playfully, taking an average of forty minutes to an hour a week, depending on the number of children involved, as well as their developmental stage (milestones the child has mastered and which still need work) (Dss.gov.au, 2020).

The facilitator is invited to use creativity and expand the topics according to the needs of each group. It is recommended that the facilitator develop this with their teams, school learning support officers (SLSOs), carers, nurses, parents, siblings and other family members. It is a systemic, participative, and interactive process.

 The main goals of the group activities include, but are not restricted to

- Creating a safe environment and positive atmosphere to promote children's self-expression

- Encouraging each child to take an active role during activities

- Promoting and strengthening individual characteristics and transitional moments within the group

- Enhancing the self-regulation of every child (Shanker, S., & Barker, T. (2017) Self-reg)

- Stimulating creative thinking and initiatives from the children

- Actively supporting social skills development

- Promoting each child to recognise, identify, name, verbalise their emotions, and learn how to share them with peers and facilitators

- Encouraging empathy - the ability to perceive other people's feelings

- Increasing and promoting the inclusion process in all schools and communities

- Navigating the gender spectrum and using various pronouns to show respect for the individual child, such as He, She, Ze, Zir, Sie, Hir, Co, Ey, and so on. ("Equal Opportunity Act", n.d)

## Family Capacity Building

This ancillary book can be used to plan weekly or monthly activities for capacity building groups with families and carers. The facilitator will play a key role in supporting parents and carers to build new skills, and enhance their knowledge and creativity.

The collaborative nature of the relationship between parents and facilitators provides learning opportunities to:

- Expand links between one another
- Encourage parents self-care
- Build capacity and emotional literacy
- Exchange strategies to best support children
- Increase play and listening skills
- Improve consistency and boundaries for children

*"When adults are supported and can model responsive relationships with each other and with children, the benefits come full circle, ultimately helping children become healthy, responsive parents themselves."* Center on the Developing Child at Harvard University (2017).

##  Behaviour Management Plan

*"No such thing as a bad kid."* – Professor Stuart Shanker

Each child is different and requires specific strategies to best support and manage their learning needs and behaviour. Children who present challenging behaviours require an assessment and, working together with family members, is necessary to define the goals that will best support their needs.

Behaviours communicate something – it is our job to investigate and understand what the child's behaviour means; why and when it occurs, and how to best assist in preventing it for that particular child. Some helpful strategies for general behaviour management, that support effective instructions, during the play group are:

- Cultivating self-care and looking after yourself.
- Using visual communication.
- Remembering you are a role model and that children are very perceptive of your emotional state. Being aware of your state of mind, your stress, your body language, your tone of voice.
- Talking about the common golden rules: from day one, it is essential to talk with children, discuss the four to five main group rules and expectations, include their ideas and make an agreement with them; it is also important to display the rules visually by using a variety of resources, such as illustrations, to support children in remembering the rules before each session.
- Encouraging peer-to-peer sharing of instructions and leadership among children.

- Being creative. The Picture Exchange Communication System (PECS) (Frost & Bondy, 2002) is one example or resource that allows children with little or no verbal or physical communication ability to communicate using pictures. You can also use signals to show what is expected at a given time, such as quieting down, starting work, and packing away materials.

- Giving children their *Are We the Same?* Activity book only when it is time for them to use them to avoid distractions.

- Organising shelves, folders, visual labels (with symbols), and containers to manage supplies.

- Utilising proactive, rather than reactive, interventions as needed; for example, planning before sessions.

- Investigating what helps a distressed child to "bounce back" quickly – each child requires their own strategies.

- Keeping a quiet corner or tent in the room to aid a child who needs space to settle and calm down.

- Speaking to a child privately about any behaviours or concerns.

- Verbalising specific, targeted positive reinforcement in public when a child meets a behavioural goal during the group. Compliments need an audience, so that the child can share their successes!

- Being a 'Sherlock Holmes'! Be aware of triggers that can set off behaviours. Sometimes these triggers are very subtle or even hidden. ("The Stressed Detective" – Self-Reg with Dr Stuart Shanker, n.d.) There may only be one trigger, or many, depending on the child. *"There is no one size fits all."*

Avoiding distractions as much as possible such as open windows, open doors, background music, TV, too much light, and people talking or eating when you are developing group dynamics. Focusing on one activity at a time, in a calm space, can be helpful for all children, in particular, for children with hyperactivity and attention disorders.

An overload of vibrant colours, posters and too much visual communication on the walls and doors can easily distract or overstimulate some children who are hypersensitive to environmental stimuli.

*"Self-regulation is concerned with how we manage stress, not inhibiting the impulses that arise from excessive stress."* Self-Reg with Dr. Stuart Shanker, 2019.

### Evaluating outcomes

Program evaluation is a systematic way to manage processes and improve results and strategies. It is encouraged to integrate evaluation with the *Are We The Same?* weekly program sessions.

The primary idea is to take corrective action when required and adapt the sessions according to your children, group, or family needs.

### Survey with children

This survey can be used with children to evaluate work at the end of the session or once a month. The survey can be presented as a one page A4 sheet featuring the four faces, as Velcro images to stick onto a board, or as coloured balls that represent each evaluation (i.e. blue for 'awesome'; orange for 'good'; yellow for 'meh' and red for 'did not like it') with four different boxes for the children to place the balls in.

The question to ask is: "How did you feel today after our play group?"

| Awesome | Good | Meh* | I didn't like it.* |
|---------|------|------|--------------------|

*If this is the response, ask why.

### Survey to use with families/teachers

In your opinion:

| QUESTIONS: | 5-Strongly Agree | 4-Agree | 3-Neutral | 2-Disagree* | 1-Strongly Disagree* |
|------------|------------------|---------|-----------|-------------|----------------------|
| The session met my expectations | | | | | |
| The facilitators communicated the workshop content effectively | | | | | |
| The program materials and visuals were well organised and easy to follow | | | | | |
| I enjoyed the interaction and participation with other carers, parents, and/or teachers | | | | | |
| What part(s) of the session did you find most useful? | | | | | |
| What can we improve? Please be specific! Thanks! ☺ | | | | | |

*If this is the response, ask why.

### Collecting data and sharing results

Before and after each session, it is important to collect data so that you can quantify and qualify changes and improvements and, if necessary, adapt the program according to your group's needs.

Examples of points to include:

- The child displayed positive social behaviour when working with peers. Before/After

- The child showed empathy and was able to cooperate with others. Before/After

- The child had emotional literacy, such as being able to identify and name the emotions they were experiencing. Before/After

- The child had self-regulation skills, such as being able to calm down independently, or seeking help when needed. Before/After

- The child was able to avoid problem behaviours, such as distress, bullying, physical, or disruptive behaviour. Before/After

- If necessary, it is suggested to access Developmental Milestones and the EYLF and NQS (Dss.gov.au, 2020). Please see at the end of this book for some links.

##  Self-awareness and setting up *self-care strategies*

*"Self-care strategies for parents are essential to address more of their feelings and emotions, how to best manage themselves in these stressful situations as well with their child."*
– Professor Stuart Shanker.

Working with children and families can be overwhelming for both the worker and the family. As facilitators, our ethical commitment is to monitor our mental health, our responses, and to ensure we are practising self-care and self-regulation strategies. Being a role model, for children and families, means that we need to be able to understand and co-regulate the child or family members – soothe, talk, listen, be with, scaffold, and withdraw when required.

These skills are only possible if we develop self-awareness and set up self-care strategies that can protect against burnout and support best practices. Remember to identify activities and practices to support and sustain your wellbeing. It can be helpful to debrief with your manager, colleagues, friends, professional supervisor or members of your family. (For more information, there are some useful links at the end of this guide.)

# Play Group

Play groups are one of the strategies used by facilitators who would like to make their teaching or learning process more creative and effective. Collaborative work is an essential aspect of a positive, interactive play group to develop social skills. Children differ in how they engage or their motivation to learn.

Because of this, the Are We The Same? project offers multiple options and sensory experiences for children to explore during the activities.

*"The use of multi-sensory education in the classroom has produced some promising results."*
Kast, Meyer, Vogeli, Gross, and Jancke, 2007.

## How to organize the groups

- **Who?** Between 10 and 15 children in each group generally works well, depending on the needs of each child and the number of SLSOs for each class.

- **When?** Once a week. Choose a day and time and make it happen! Consistency is key - children rely on our consistency and, after a while, they will come to expect the *Are We The Same?* play group to take place at a certain time.

- **How long?** 40-60 minutes, depending on the age of the group and settings where it will be developed.

- **Where?** In a space with tables and chairs (removable or foldable), plenty of art and craft materials, a white board, music, yoga mats, cushions, sensory toys, and a mini sensory space such as a tent, for any situation where children need a moment to self-regulate or calm down.

- **What?** Activities with *Are We The Same?* book.

*"Belonging is central to being and becoming in that it shapes who children are and who they can become."* The Early Years Learning Framework (EYLF) - (COAG) 2009.

**Play group golden rules**

An agreement needs to be made between the children and facilitators in the first play group session and before every other session starts.

Use visual resources during the group sessions and talk about these 'golden rules', including photos and images for any Augmentative and Alternative Communication (AAC), Key Word Signs (KWS), Picture Exchange Communication System (PECS) or similar systems, to provide extra support for children with a very limited or unintelligible speech. You may require use of a communication device to promote communication and encourage all participation and innovative ideas.

Stick the golden rules on a wall to read through with the children before the start of every session.

 **Listen** - When someone is talking, we are listening. When we are talking, others are listening.

 **Respect** - We keep our hands to ourselves. We respect each other's space, feelings and thoughts.

 **Participate** - Your opinion is important! Let us play and enjoy our time together!

 **Ask for help** - If you need help, ask! (Facilitators can provide visual resources or cards to children so they can ask for help).

Talk or show a "help card" to a teacher, facilitator, or SLSO every time someone is injured or not feeling well, whether people are fighting or something else is disrupting the group harmony in some way. In these cases, we can stop our activity and talk about finding solutions together.

 **Let us use kind and "magic words" to learn how to play together -** We ask nicely by saying 'please', 'sorry' and 'thank you'. We learn to share and to make choices. We learn how to give other people a chance to play.

 **Take a break -** it is okay if you need it, just ask! (Note: if someone is finding things difficult or is not feeling well during an activity, we will try to help. Otherwise, we respect that the person might need some time to rest and feel calm again.)

 **Relax! -** This can be in the "calm tent", "pea pod", or other soothing sensory resource (for any situation where children need a moment to self-regulate or remove themselves from too many stimuli – to learn how to calm down).

The child can also go outside or to another room with a facilitator, teacher or SLSO, where it will be more relaxed and quieter. The child may wish to use sensory toys. This especially applies in the case of children who need high support, whether they are distressed and/or displaying stressed or challenging behaviours.

 **New ideas?** - Ask children to add new rules or suggestions!

# The Role of the Facilitator

*"The facilitator role is one of improving a group's communication and information flow; facilitators are meant to enhance the manner in which a group makes decisions without making those decisions for the group."* Griffith, Fuller, and Northcraft, 1998.

**Remember!** Facilitators avoid biasing the group with their own opinions. Facilitators will use different resources to stimulate all children to blend in, using alternative learning styles: visual (objects, photos, drawings), auditory (music, sounds), kinaesthetic (physical exercise, dancing, moving around). (Judy, B. 2010.)

- **Logistic**: Help yourself and prepare an agenda, logistic, and process before each session.

- **Introductions**: Make sure the group knows your name and your role. Take time to have all participants introduce themselves. Use badges!

- **Be positive**: Serve as a positive force in the group, setting the tone so the best solutions can be found. Your role is to facilitate children to seek solutions and clear any doubts or any issues about topics the group will discuss.

- **Remain neutral**: Support the group to develop a creative thinking process. If you have valuable ideas or opinions that are essential to the discussion, add your input AFTER the children give theirs.

- **Keep the focus**: Ensure children's focus remains on the task related to the subject of the day.

- **Encourage participation**: Encourage all children to participate by monitoring excessive talkers and encouraging the quieter members. Solve any behavioural issues that interfere with the group's processes.

- **Protect ideas**: Always protect individuals and their ideas with respectful comments, this reduces the likelihood of attack from others. Observe bullying attitudes and/or behaviours by members of the group. 'No bullying' is a ground rule that everyone is asked to follow and to understand what it means.

- **Avoid criticising or evaluate ideas**: Creative ideas will be suggested. Instead of evaluating these ideas, encourage contributors to explain the background behind their ideas.

- **Work with a recorder (or scribe)**: You will be busy facilitating, so have someone else record the sessions or use the information to prepare a group summary memo for yourself. Write or draw main points while working with the children!

- **Visual support**: Visual resources help children to memorise and learn. As far as possible, use visual resources to improve receptive and expressive communication (Bondy, A. &, F.L. 2002). For example, stick flip chart paper around the class and use it to write-on during sessions. Remove it only after all children have left the room. (Bondy, A.) The same process may be used with parents.

- **Evaluation/feedback**: Remember to ask for feedback at the end of each session. Discuss what is working, what is not working, what can be improved, and request ideas and feedback from the children.

 ## Experiential learning cycle

Experiential learning occurs when someone (child, family or professionals) "engages in an activity, looks back at the activity critically, gains some useful insight from the analysis, and promotes behaviour changes in accordance with the results" (Kolb & Fry, 1975).

*"As far as possible, use multiple modalities, and help children respond to learning with a variety of assessment tools".* Universal Design for Learning (UDL), 2019

 ## Play Group: how does it work?

There are four distinct sections to the play group and it is important to respect these sections to build trust and organise each different task. When the group starts, we explain the day's theme. Each activity is explained by the facilitator, before the game begins. Ask the group to sit in a large circle and explain the ideas!

The four sections of the play group are:

 **Ice breaking (IB)**: This comprises the first 15 minutes of the session depending on the age of the children. The facilitator develops fun games with music (which is essential to increase productivity in the group). This is a high-energy fun way to start the session and helps the people in the group to learn each other's names, get to know one another, and let go of inhibitions.

 **Activity/Theme of the day** (**DA**): 25 to 30 minutes. The facilitator promotes self-awareness activities with different strategies relevant to the theme of the day, including exercises to develop self-awareness, trust, and team-work values.

 **Relaxation (RLX)**: 5 to 10 minutes. Children collaborate in the organisation of mats, cushions, and blankets. With everyone in the group sitting or lying down with their eyes closed and relaxing music in the background, the facilitator helps everyone listen to the sounds of nature or shares a brief story. Another option is that children are guided step by step to body relaxation.

 **Closing activity (CA):** In the last 5 minutes, in a circle, the mediator encourages each child (if they wish) to share their own feelings with the group before they leave the room.

 ### Material required:

Besides the *Are We The Same?* book, most sessions will require basic stationary resources, such as A4 and large colourful papers, kraft paper roll, markers, scissors, glue, magazines, colourful texters pencils, glitter, laminated art crafts supplies, colour tape, yoga mats, cushions, tent and audio visual resources for example a TV to play videos and music. When it is required, specific material will be mentioned in the descriptions of the activity.

**Remember:** Make the most of each session!

*"Whatever you do, do it well."* — Walt Disney

This auxiliary book was created to provide tools to the facilitator, to teach perspective-taking skills that enable all children to gain insight into how others feel and to develop a sense of social responsibility towards one another.

Parents, teachers, SLSOs and school staff help children to learn positive social skills by modelling or being positive examples for children to follow. Guiding children and providing opportunities for them to express their feelings and ideas, to learn new skills, and to practise what they have learnt, will help them to make and keep friends using positive social skills.

Key social skills that help with friendships include being able to listen, to cooperate, to communicate what they need or want, to have empathy, to learn core concepts involved in Theory of Mind (Kloo et al., 2010), to have emotional intelligence and self-control, and to take responsibility for themselves (for example, organising their own toys) (Ue Larkey & Gay von Ess, 2016).

# Are We the Same?
## Activities, Ideas & Themes:
## Part 1

Let's introduce each other and learn about abilities and disabilities.

| THEME #1 | WHAT DO I EXPECT TO DO DURING OUR GROUP TIME? |
| --- | --- |
| GOAL | Raise children's expectations about this therapeutic play group. |
| STRATEGIES | **IB** - Holding hands in a circle, facing the centre, everyone in the group jumps in, out, left, or right of the circle, coordinated with your instructions (circle made with colour tape on the floor).<br><br>**DA** - Informal chat with the children about their expectations and the themes they would like to work on during the year. The facilitator writes or draws everything on a board or paper.<br><br>**RLX** - With music or story about "animals' transformations".<br><br>**Closing Activity -** Which animal did you choose to be? |

| THEME #2 | DRAWING YOURSELF |
| --- | --- |
| GOAL | Self-image, self-perception, and perception of others.<br>Specific material required: Safety mirror for children. |
| STRATEGIES | **IB** - Statues: start the music and the children can 'go nuts' dancing and being silly. Stop the music and all the children must freeze in whatever position they are in. Watch the children for any movement – the first person to move goes out. Then restart the music and repeat until only one person is left.<br><br>**DA** - Use the mirror to promote self-perception of personal characteristics and perceptions of all colleagues. Talk about the similarities and differences observed. The participants will draw self-portraits. It is always a fun way to get to know each other and ourselves!<br><br>**RLX** - Let us imagine how many stars there are in the sky!<br><br>**Closing Activity -** What colour are the stars that you imagined? |

**THEME #3** LET US MEET OUR GROUP?

**GOAL**

Start inclusion conversation.

Specific material required: Balloons and ribbons.

**STRATEGIES**

 **IB** - Dancing with balloons. The players inflate their balloon and use yarn to attach it to their foot or leg. The balloon should be attached so it does not get in the way of the person dancing, but is close enough to the floor so others have the opportunity to step on it. The players then spread on the "dance floor". Once the music starts, all the players try to jump on the balloons of the other participants. When a player loses his balloon, he has to leave the dance floor. The last player with an intact balloon wins the game.

 **DA** - Introduction and free colouring of characters.

**RLX** - Relaxation in pairs. Children sit back to back with a partner in a cross-legged position (using support if desired). Take a few deep breaths, in silence or with music, and focus on feeling your partner's breathing.

# Are We the Same?
# Activities, Ideas & Themes:
# Part 2

**THEME #4**

**TAKING CARE OF MY BODY AND MYSELF!**

 **GOAL**

Looking at self-care, personal hygiene, taking care of oneself, and being healthy.

**STRATEGIES**

 **IB** - Chair game. The game starts with any number of players and one less chair than the players. The chairs are arranged in a circle (or other closed figure if space is constrained - a double line is sometimes used) facing outward, with the children standing in a circle just outside of that. A facilitator plays recorded music or a musical instrument. While the music is playing, those in the circle walk around the chairs. When the facilitator stops the music, everyone must race to sit on one of the chairs. The person left without a chair is eliminated from the game. One chair is removed to ensure there are still more players than chairs. The music resumes and the cycle repeats until there is only one player left in the game, the winner.

 **DA** - Collage. In two groups, children choose pictures in magazines about things we use for our own self-care and hygiene. The groups then make collages on cardboard using the pictures. Each group then presents their collage to the other group.

 **RLX** - With music, the facilitator tells the story of "Traveling Into The Clouds".

 **Closing Activity** - What did you see in your cloud?

---

 **THEME #5**

**LET'S TALK ABOUT OUR FAMILIES (RELATIONSHIPS)**

 **GOAL**

Identify similarities, differentiate various types of families (single parents, same sex parents, foster families, etc.), and understand our feelings about them according to the children's questions.

**STRATEGIES**

 **IB** - Children dance around the room, before stopping over an "X" placed at various locations on the floor with colour tape. Gradually, the facilitator removes each "X", one by one, until only one remains, and everyone is together on the same "X".

 **DA** - The facilitator divides the children into two random groups. The children make collages using magazine images of various types of families. Each group then presents their collage to the other group.

 **RLX** - With relaxation music, the children lie down on cushions or mats and the facilitator tells the story of "The Journey Of A Bird".

 **Closing Activity -** What colour is your bird?

**THEME #6**

**WHAT DO I LIKE/DISLIKE? (2 SESSIONS)**

**GOAL**

 Raise personal opinions and feelings in the group, outline tastes and preferences, differentiate individuality, and enhance self-perception.

Specific materials required: Multi-coloured cotton ball or marshmallow.

**STRATEGIES**

 **IB** - The facilitator draws a moon, a sun, or a star on the back of each child's hand. Read the story "The Moon, The Sun And The Star". Each child stands and spins around when the character corresponding to their drawing is mentioned.

 **DA** - The facilitator promotes open discussion about the children's views and perceptions about what they love/like (food, toys, feelings, colours). As each child expresses their views, the facilitator draws a picture of their suggestion on the board. Once the board has been filled with drawings of the children's suggestions, each child is then invited to colour in a paper heart with their favourite colour.

 **RLX** - With music and a story about "The Fairy Who Gave A Drop Of Love To Each Child". (You can research the suggested stories or make up stories of your own.)

 **Closing Activity** - Each child should make a bowl shape with his hand to receive the drop of love (a multi-coloured cotton ball or a marshmallow).

---

**THEME #7**

**WHAT ARE THE SEVEN DIFFERENCES?**

**GOAL**

 The concept of differences.

Specific material required: colourful ribbons.

**STRATEGIES**

 **IB** - In two groups, children 'freeze' in various poses. One group walks around to notice the differences between each pose. The groups then swap over.

 **DA** - Let us find the seven differences.

 **RLX:** The facilitator reads the "Green World Story".

 **Closing Activity** - Each child receives a colourful star at the end of the activity. You can make the stars yourself or buy them at a craft shop.

He, She, Ze, Zir: HOW DO YOU SEE YOURSELF?

## GOAL

The two gender identities most people are familiar with are 'boy' and 'girl'. In addition to these two identities, other identities are now commonplace.

Fluidity: Gender is an expression of our self. It is the way we show who we are to the world, through such things as clothing and hairstyles. The facilitator will talk about this subject according to the children's level of questions. By age three, most children prefer activities and exhibit behaviours typically associated with their assigned gender, but this is not true for all children. However, children who express themselves outside of the binary (boy/girl) genders often have a very different experience. Navigating pronouns while respecting any child's choice is an inclusive attitude. By using He, She, Ze, Zir and so on, it is possible to promote a better understanding of gender identity and the gender spectrum. (Gender Neutral Pronouns | LGBT Resource Center | USC", n.d.)

Please check the free course, "Health Across the Gender Spectrum" by Stanford University: https://www.coursera.org/learn/health-gender-spectrum

## STRATEGIES

 **IB**: Musical Chairs: The game starts with any number of participants and one less chair than the participants. The chairs are arranged in a circle or a double line, with the seats facing outward, and with the class standing in front of the chairs. The facilitator plays recorded music or a musical instrument. While the music is playing, the children walk in single file around the chairs. When the music stops, everyone must race to sit down on one of the chairs. The person who is left without a chair is eliminated from the game. A chair is removed to ensure there is still one less chair than the number of participants. The music resumes and the cycle repeats until there is only one participant left in the game. This person is the winner.

 **DA -** Draw pictures on the blackboard about choices and preferences. Facilitator has to be very careful to avoid gender stereotypes and own beliefs. Draw pictures on different sheets of paper showing different people grouped according to their gender.

 **RLX -** A guided body relaxation accompanied by music.

 **Closing Activity -** Each child receives a colourful ribbon at the end of the activity to represent the rainbow and the gender spectrum (multicoloured, not only blue and pink).

Session movies. As part of a weekly schedule, especially for this module, you can use some scenes from films to help illustrate your points. Suggestions: "Dolphin Tale", "Toy Story", "Teletubbies", "Shark Tale", "Shrek", "SheZow" (aged 7 and above), "Lilo and Stitch".

In groups, the children discuss what they learned from the film scenes and create drawings of their choosing about the topic.

**THEME #9**  BEING CREATIVE OR COPY OTHERS. WHAT'S THE DIFFERENCE?

**GOAL**  Encourage individuality and creativity. Introduce concepts of discrimination (me and others).

**STRATEGIES**

 **IB**: Simon Says: One participant takes the role of "Simon" and issues instructions (usually physical actions such as "jump in the air" or "stick out your tongue") to the other participants, which should only be followed if prefaced with the phrase "Simon says". For example, "Simon says, jump in the air."

Players are eliminated from the game by either failing to follow an instruction which is prefixed by the phrase "Simon says" or by following an instruction that is not prefixed by the phrase "Simon says".

It is the ability to distinguish between valid and invalid commands, rather than physical ability, that usually matters in this game. In most cases, the action just needs to be attempted.

 **DA** - Talk about being original and copying others, such as in the "Simon Says" game.

Tell a story and invent two different endings (the story can be acted out with the two different endings performed by two different groups).

Tell the traditional story of "Little Red Riding Hood", using puppets. Then divide the children into two groups and invite them to invent different endings.

The groups take turns to perform their story with the puppets.

 **RLX** - Tell the story of "Little Fairy Tinkerbell" with white music playing in the background.

**Closing Activity** - Each child receives a little "magic fairy dust" in the palm of their hand to do whatever he or she wants with. You can use glitter for the magic fairy dust.

| | |
|---|---|
| **THEME #10** |  WHY ARE PEOPLE DIFFERENT? |
| **GOAL** |  Promote self-perception and self-image, identify and discern common personal traits held by the group, and also divergent ones.<br><br>Specific material required: cotton ball cloud and glitter (you can buy these from craft shops or make them yourself). |
| **STRATEGIES** |  **IB** - The "Never Three Game". When the music stops, the children need to form groups, but never comprised of three people, or they will be eliminated.<br><br> **DA** - After talking about the individuality of each child, the children are randomly divided into two groups.<br><br>The groups then look for different people in magazines (distinguished by race, religion, size, shape, gender, culture, and so on) and use the images to make a collage on cardboard. Each group then presents its collage to the other group.<br><br>**RLX** - Tell the story of "The Little Magic Bubble Ball".<br><br>**Closing Activity** - Each child receives a colourful cotton ball cloud and glitter raindrops. |

| | |
|---|---|
| **THEME #11** |  ABILITY AND DISABILITY. WHAT DO THEY MEAN? (Divide this subject into four fortnightly sessions interspersed with other topics, see 1-4 below) |
| **GOAL** |  Assess personal feelings, biases, myths and fantasies. Identify similarities and differences. Encourage respect and promote empathy. Promote the ability to express emotions productively (Steiner, 2003). Conceptual construction of respectful and correct terminology for people with disabilities.<br><br>Specific material required: blindfolds. |
| **STRATEGIES** |  **IB** - Each child chooses a balloon. Music is played, and the children play with their balloons, following commands such as, 'Play alone, play in pairs, play in threes, everyone play together.'<br><br> **DA** - 1) Physical disability. In silence, using wheelchairs, walking frames, walking stick and crutches, the children experience what it would be like to have a physical disability. The children are divided into two groups. One group of children guides the other group, before switching roles. As a whole class group, the children discuss how they felt about the experience and create drawings of their choosing about the subject. |

2) Sensory experiences (visual disability). Using blindfolds, the children experience what it would be like to have a visual disability. The children are split into two groups. One group are blindfolded and the sighted children guide the blindfolded children (one to one), before switching roles. As a whole class group, the children discuss how they felt about the experience and create drawings of their choosing about the subject.

3) Mimic game (hearing disability). 'Mimic' can be a fun memory game that improves the children's ability for recall and builds their capacity to make accurate guesses about what people are talking about using body language, gestures or signs. The game is required to be played in silence. As a whole class group, the children discuss how they felt about the experience and create drawings of their choosing about the subject.

4) Intellectual disability. Two versions of the same story are told. One is told using only photos and the other is told using only words. The aim is to help the children understand that people learn in different ways and that sometimes we change the ways we say things to make it easier for others to understand. The facilitator explains that intellectual disability means that someone learns and develops differently than others.

5) Session movies. As part of a weekly schedule, especially for this module, you can use some scenes from films to help illustrate your points. Suggestions: "Nemo", "Wonder", "The Hunchback of Notre Dame", "Dolphin Tale", "Avatar", "Toy Story", "ET", "Teletubbies", "Beauty and the Beast", " Shark Tale", "Maleficent", "Shaun the Sheep", "Shrek", "SheZow" (aged 7 and above), "Lilo and Stitch", and "Soul Surfer".

In groups, the children discuss what they learned from the film scenes and create drawings of their choosing about the topics.

**RLX** - Children listen to new age music with nature sounds. They try to discern the various different sounds, such as birds, ocean, wind in the leaves, and create a picture in their mind.

**Closing Activity** - In a circle, each child will share what or who they imagined (their fantasies).

# Are We the Same?
## Activities, Ideas & Themes:
## Part 3

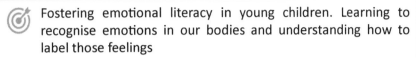

**THEME #12**

  WHEN I AM UNHAPPY AND WHEN I AM HAPPY (2 SESSIONS)

**GOAL**

  Fostering emotional literacy in young children. Learning to recognise emotions in our bodies and understanding how to label those feelings

Specific material required: Positive stickers or smiley stars.

**STRATEGIES**

  **IB** - Dance game. With energetic music playing, all children start to dance. When the volume of the music is turned down the children start to walk on 'all fours' with their hands and feet on the floor.

  **DA** - Step by step, we talk about what makes us unhappy and happy. The children create drawings of their choosing on two separate sheets of paper, one for each feeling, to represent both joyous and sad experiences they have had.

**Extra resource**: Depending on children's age, play scenes from movies, for example, "Inside Out" and "Maleficent" – include the scene where she loses her wings, then gets them back and flies free.

  **RLX** - "Growing Smiles" (poem for kids).

  **Closing Activity** - Each child receives a colourful 'smile star' at the end of the activity (you can make these yourself or buy them at craft shops).

---

**THEME #13**

  AHHHH! A FEAR OF FEAR!

WOW! HOW BRAVE I AM!

**GOAL**

  Fostering emotional literacy in young children. Recognising emotions in our bodies and learning to label these feelings.

Talk about situations, real or imagined, that cause fear. Talk about how to take a positive approach and find solutions to overcome these fears and scenarios.

Specific material required: double-sided circle of paper (you can make these yourself or you can buy them from craft shops and write the words using different coloured pens).

**STRATEGIES**

**IB -** Funny dancing game. Prompt children to dance facing each other, then facing away from each other, and so on.

**DA** - Talk about the things that we fear. This could be scary movies, animals, people or situations.

Draw pictures of the fear: What colour is fear? What does it look like? How does it appear in our imaginations?

Talk about bullying and fear. Talk about the fear of telling the truth, blaming others, and so on. Talk about how all emotions are valid.

Then draw something that can take away the fear — courage! What does it feel like to have courage? What is it like to be brave? What colour is courage?

**RLX** - With music playing, tell the story of "Big Fear and Small Fear".

**Closing Activity** - Each child receives a colourful double-sided circle of paper with 'courage' written on one side and 'fear' written on the other side.

Movie option. Play scenes from "Inside Out" or "Dumbo".

**THEME #14**

WHY DON'T I WANT TO TALK MY FRIEND? (THE SILENT TREATMENT AND TEMPER TANTRUMS) WHY DO I FEEL LIKE THIS? WHAT IS THE SOLUTION?

**GOAL**

Assess self-perception, personal limits, tolerance, emotional distress, and frustration. Problem solving skills. Recognise emotions in our bodies and understand how to label these feelings - identify anger, respect, and encourage empathy.

**STRATEGIES**

**IB -** Red Light, Green Light game: Clearly define the playing area with designated 'start' and 'finish' lines. Begin the game with everyone lined up along the start line. When you say, "Green Light", everyone moves towards the finish line. When you say, "Red Light", everyone must immediately stop.

If players are still moving when you call "Red Light", they must go back to the start line. Begin a new round once everyone gets across the finish line or when one player makes it across the finish line.

**DA** - Children with sulky faces. How we react when we cannot have our own way? How do we solve this problem?

**RLX** - Children's relaxation (ocean music or similar white nature sounds).

**Closing Activity** - Movie option: Play scenes from "Inside Out".

**GOAL**

 Feelings and intentions. Work on self-perception and empathy stimulation. Find solutions to help others without invading their personal space. Talk about 'Space invaders' and how to avoid it. Respect other people's right to say no. Set agreed boundaries.

Specifc material required: rounded plastic chopstcks or straws (quills), porcupine stickers (paper or plastc).

**STRATEGIES**

 **IB - Option 1:** Crows and Cranes. Using a flat, two-sided object, such as a frisbee, divide the group into two teams, the crows and the cranes. Gently throw the object into the air.

When the object lands on one side, the crows chase the cranes. When the object lands on the other side, the cranes chase the crows. The teams start facing each other as a line is designated behind each team as the 'goal'. If the crows chase the cranes, the cranes have to get past their line before they are tagged. If they are tagged, they become a crow. This can last FOREVER!

 **IB - Option 2:** The Story of Prickles The Porcupine: Ask the group to form a circle, you included. All participants follow the instructions of the story.

Explore this story as a group exercise, developing a role play with the children.

The children can dramatize the story, using rounded plastic chopsticks or straws to represent the porcupine quills (but keep enough distance between the children, so that no one gets hurt!). You also can use the music Space Invaders (YouTube/1980).

Exploring personal space is fun, talk about space invaders to develop communication and social skills! Discuss how the emotions felt within their body and what feelings they can name.

**DA -** The rule is that whilst doing this activity it is helpful for teaching children about how close is too close when interacting with others.

Learn to respect other people's space and boundaries, independence, and choices. Get input from the children about how this makes them feel and some solutions. (Use Solution Organizer - Problem solving skills sheet at the end of the book if you wish). Talk about the bubble we can have around ourselves that keeps us safe in our personal space. Provide paper for the children to draw on. Invite them to draw pictures of how they can support each other while telling them a story on the subject.

**RLX** - Chatty Sheep or The Magic Tree: Good manners. (http://freestoriesforkids.com/audiosto ries/american-english/magic-tree-audio-story-kids-music-and-sound-effects

https://freestoriesforkids.com/children/stories-and-tales/magic-tree)

**Closing Activity** - Place a little spaceship sticker/or porcupine sticker in the palm of each child's hand.

Other resources: Work with hula hoops is fantastic and very visual for the children – each child can have one as a personal bubble, the children can set some rules and all play with music around the class or outdoors.

Also check some videos on YouTube: "Personal Space a Social Story".

(https://youtu.be/MGQzDfbwWko
https://youtu.be/VL1kZugHuUI)

---

**THEME #16**

HOW CAN I OFFER MY HELP OR IDEAS?

**GOAL**

Active support principle. Share reactions and observations. Recognise emotions in our body and identify the feelings (such as anxiety or frustration). Differentiate 'me' from 'other'.

Talk about how to respond when someone steps over our personal boundaries. Ask first! Avoid guessing or assuming what is alright for other people.

Specific material required: Large physiotherapy colourful bands.

**STRATEGIES**

**IB** - Accompanied by music, the children dance around. When the facilitator says, "Face To Face", the children stop dancing and stand facing one another. When the facilitator says, "Back to Back", the children stop dancing and stand back to back. The children should continually change pairs throughout the game until they've all exchanged pairs.

**DA** - The children are invited to make drawings for one another. Working in pairs, they ask the other child what they would like a picture of and then draw the requested picture for the other child. On a separate piece of paper each child draws a picture of their choosing. The children can then compare what they have drawn.

The facilitator talks to the children about their drawing, boundaries, and how to set boundaries that everybody feels comfortable with.

**RLX** - Working in pairs, the children relax using a large resistant physiotherapy band.

**Closing Activity** - Read the poem "Love Respects" (at the end of this book).

**THEME #17**

 **WHAT DOES IT MEAN TO BE A FRIEND?**

 **GOAL**

Share feelings and fantasies, identify the qualities of those whom we call our friends, differentiate types of friends, classmates, and strangers.

**STRATEGIES**

 **IB** - Limbo-Irish Rope Dance. Accompanied by music, the children dance under a rope or bar without touching it. After everyone has passed under the bar or rope, it is lowered and the next round of the game begins. If you touch the bar, you need to wait until a new game begins.

**DA** - Chat about the meaning of being a friend, and the differences between friends, not friends and strangers. Warn about strangers and speak about the dangers they can present and what strangers are safe to ask help (such as firefighters, police). Each child draws his or her best friend in their workbook.

**RLX** - In pairs, the children work with play dough to make something special for their friend or classmate.

**Closing Activity -** Body relaxation. Accompanied by "You've Got A Friend In Me" from the Toy Story soundtrack.

---

 **THEME #18**

 **HOW DO I SPEAK TO OTHERS?**

 **GOAL**

Fostering emotional literacy in young children. Recognising emotions and learning how to label those feelings. Improving self-perception, empathy, and creating strategies for self-control and learn to use kind words to each other.

**STRATEGIES**

 **IB** - Everybody walks around the room clapping. When the facilitator says "Two!", the children form a pair. When the facilitator says "Three!", the children group in threes, and so on, until all children are together in one group.

**DA** - In two groups, the children create scenes with characters. The characters talk in different ways, such as loudly, quietly, politely, whispering and shouting. One group will be the other group's audience. Explain that the children need to use the magic words, "Please", "Thank you", and "I am sorry" when needed.

**RLX** - The children listen to The Chatty Sheep (https://freestoriesforkids.com/children/stories-and-tales/chatty-sheep)

**Closing Activity -** Relaxation accompanied by nature meditation music.

Depending on the age of the children, you can use this video: "How To Say Please, Thank You And Sorry Song"

https://www.youtube.com/watch?v=Mx0mNNaWeOg

**THEME #19**

**LEARN HOW TO LISTEN**

**GOAL**

 Improve the ability to communicate and listen.

**STRATEGIES**

 **IB** - The Mirror Game. Divide the group into pairs. Choose one person in each pair to lead and the other will follow. The partners sit facing each other and the leader begins to make large, slow movements that the follower will imitate as if the leader is the follower's own reflection in a mirror. After a while, switch over, so that the leader becomes the follower and vice versa.

 **DA** - Using puppets, tell the story "Talk Talk Talk", in which all the puppets talk at the same time, but do not listen to each other. After telling the story, ask the children how they feel about it. Ask how they would help the puppets. Using their workbooks, invite the children to draw how the story made them feel.

 **RLX** - With white music featuring birdsong, frogs croaking, crickets chirping, wind whistling, and water splashing, help the children notice the different sounds.

 **Closing Activity** - What did you hear? Which sound did you like the most?

---

**THEME #20**

 BABIES, TODDLERS AND PRESCHOOL CHILDREN. WHAT IS THE DIFFERENCE?

**GOAL**

 Self-perception. Differentiate between "what I am" and "what I'm not". Differentiate between how babies, toddlers and preschool children communicate. Explore personal resources and self-regulation skills. This enables a child to move from depending on others to beginning to manage by themselves, learning how to express when they are tired, hungry, having sensory issues, and how they feel during transitions or when facing new experiences.

When these things happen, they might become upset, sulky or angry. Teach strategies to help children to learn to regulate their behaviour.

Specific material required: little squeeze ball or small squeeze animal for each child.

**IB** - With background music, the facilitator says the name of a body part such as "Ear!" The children dance with their hands on their ears. Then the facilitator calls out another body part, such as "Legs!", and the children dance with their hands on their legs, and so on.

 **DA** - Invite the children to draw pictures of babies, toddlers, and preschool children. Talk with the children about what they can do to manage their emotions, such as, "When I feel (angry, upset, and so on) I can (suggest sensory strategies such as squeezing a ball, counting to ten, breathing slowly, listening to music, walk away, dancing).

Discuss how each age group of children, from babies up to preschool children, tend to react to stressors, their differences and similarities, and self-regulation strategies.

 **RLX** - With music playing quietly in the background, the children relax in pairs.

 **Closing Activity -** Each child receives a little squeezable rubber ball.

---

 WHERE DID I COME FROM? HOW WAS I BORN? (2 SESSIONS)

 The most positive method of responding to the "Where do we come from?" question may be to encourage the child to think for him/herself.

Essentially, the idea would be to spark a conversation on the topic according to the child's age and questions.

 **IB** - Back To Back. Working in pairs, the children stand back to back. The facilitator gives the children different instructions that they must try to follow while staying back to back.

The instructions will be things such as "right hand to left hand", "left foot to right foot", "head to head", "right hand to left leg" and so on, and the children must touch these body parts together.

The pairs continue to follow these instructions until the facilitator calls "Back to Back", at which point the children switch partners. If you have an odd number of participants, the extra child can assist the facilitator.

 **DA** - Chat about life. Discuss how we are born and encourage ideas from the kids. Draw pictures of pregnant women. Have a few baby dolls available for the children to look at and play with.

 **RLX** - Tell a story, "My mum is having a baby" or "I am going to have a new little brother or sister". There are many books on this subject, so choose your favourite.

**Closing Activity -** The children relax on yoga mats or cushions while listening to nursery songs.

**MY NEW LITTLE BROTHER**

 Fostering emotional literacy in young children. Recognising emotions and learning how to label these feelings. Encourage children to talk about jealousy and their feelings about having a new baby at home. When and why do we feel jealous?

Specific material required: Glitter Confetti Glitter Metallic Foil Stars.

 **IB** - Peek-A-Who? Split the group into two teams. A bed sheet is held up by two adults. Each team sits behind one side of the sheet, hidden from the other team. One child from each team sits facing the sheet. When the sheet is lowered, the first team that says the name of the child on the opposite side gets that player on their team. The game ends when everyone is on the same side.

 **DA** - Talk about who has a new baby at home, or who knows someone who has a new baby. How do they feel about it? Invite the children to draw a picture of "my new brother".

 **RLX** - Tell the story of "The Jealousy Kingdom And The Happy Kingdom"; you can look at the internet for stories on this theme or make one up yourself.

 **Closing Activity** - The children all receive glitter or metallic foil stars to share with their friends or their brothers and sisters.

---

 **COPYCAT**

Share emotions about how we copy others and why we do it! How can we do things differently? Ask the children to think of different ways to show someone that they want to be their friend.

 **IB** - Competition. Dance the same dance differently! First, perform an action such as stamping your foot while dancing. Then, stamping your foot again, ask, "Did I do the SAME thing or something DIFFERENT?"

Once the children have answered, say, "Let's all do the SAME thing!". Once all the children have stamped their feet while dancing, say, "Let's all do something DIFFERENT!"

At this point, each child creates their own dance. The most original dancer will win a special prize! The prize can be anything, such as a piece of fruit or a little toy.

**DA** - Discuss with children about their experience. Ask them to reflect on their behaviour during the copycat activity and why some people need to copy.

After the group discussion, invite the children to draw a picture of their choosing about the story.

Help children who have a need to copy others to understand why they copy and, if copying, discuss the importance of choosing positive behaviours to copy. In time, they will come to see the benefits and perform those behaviours on their own.

 **RLX** - With meditation or white music playing in the background, ask the children to imagine their own favourite flower or fruit.

 **Closing Activity -** Each child shares a description of their flower or fruit with the rest of the group.

---

**THEME #24**

**GOAL**

**STRATEGIES**

CHOICES

 Working with a child-centred model, explore choices and child-lead play.

**IB** - All the children sit in a circle. The facilitator starts to tell a story, then asks one of the children to continue. The storytelling continues to pass from child to child around the circle, with each child adding their own contribution, until it gets back to the first child. The facilitator then ends the story.

 **DA** - Ask the children to think about something that they would like to eat, something they would like to drink, something they would like to wear, and a place that they would like to visit.

Then ask them if it was difficult or easy to make these choices. Invite the children to draw pictures of their choices.

 **RLX** - Read a poem about choices.

 **Closing Activity** - Each child makes a choice about whether they would like to take a yellow paper star or a red paper star as a gift. Ensure there are enough of each for the children to have the colour of their choice.

RESPONSIBILITY? WHAT IT MEANS?

## GOAL

 Explore concepts of self-care, independence, and responsibility for looking after our own bodies; as well as looking after our school, our family and our planet.

Specific materials required: Colourful glitter. Blindfolds. Recommended setting: outdoors, in a location with no dangerous obstacles.

## STRATEGIES

 **IB** - Trust Walk Activity. Team-building activity centred around trust and responsibility. A leader gives verbal or nonverbal instructions to navigate a blindfolded person to avoid obstacles.

Form pairs. Ask one partner to be the navigator (guide) and the other to be blindfolded.

When the blindfolded partner is ready, the guide should not touch the partner but rely solely on verbal cues (e.g. "About five steps ahead, there is a branch. Step over it slowly").

The child guide is responsible for their partner's safety and should navigate to avoid simple obstacles. In this way, participants learn valuable lessons related to teamwork and the responsibility of caring for another individual's well-being, while the blindfolded partner learns to trust and rely on another person.

 **DA** - Ask children to reflect and share upon their experiences.

What was it like to be the guide responsible for the safety of your teammates?

How does this relate to our playgroup? Have an interactive talk with the children about being responsible for oneself and for others. Invite the children to make collages on the theme using pictures cut from magazines.

 **RLX** - Tell the story or play a scene of "Frozen", "Mulan", "Toy Story" or "Peter Pan".

**Closing Activity** - Give each child a sprinkling of magic dust (glitter).

**WHAT IS TEAMWORK? (TWO OR THREE SESSIONS)**

 Promoting the ability to work together with others as part of a team is not simply a skill needed at school, it is a vital skill used in all areas of life. School is, however, an excellent time to cultivate the teamwork ethos. Children will then draw on these early experiences throughout their lives.

Learning to work cooperatively with others towards a shared purpose. Respecting each other's abilities and opinions. Exchanging ideas and actions. Moving from more intrapersonal (individual) ways of thinking to interpersonal (communicating with others) ways of thinking.

 **IB/DA** -

Session 1: Magazine photo hunt.

Divide children in small groups. They have to find photos in magazines. Have the children work together on a project – it could be anything from a collective art project, such as creating a collage or puppet-making to performing a play.

Encourage all the children to work together in small groups to decide on their roles in the team.

Session 2: Amazing race!

The facilitator divides the children into two teams and sets them a task, such as putting all their schoolbags together in a pile. The first team to complete the task are the winners.

Session 3: Play scenes from a movie about teamwork, such as "Ants", "Finding Nemo" or "The Secret Life of Pets".

 Have a group discussion about teamwork after the children have watched the scenes.

 **SELF- EVALUATION**

Promote awareness of self-perception and self-improvement.

We can use this resource to support children to build self-perception, with five criteria: Great, Good, Average, Below Average, and Oh No! or There is room for improvement!

Children then will evaluate themselves with the smiley, neutral or sad faces:

WHY DO I HAVE TO GO TO SCHOOL?

**GOAL**

 Talk about the importance of having goals, studying and following our dreams/choices for what we want to do when we grow up.

**STRATEGIES**

 **IB** - Seagulls and Crows Game.

Split the group into two teams. Assign one team to be the 'crows' and the other to be the 'seagulls'.

The teams line up in the middle of the room facing towards each other with about three feet between them.

Explain the rules, which are as follows: You will be telling a story. If you say the word "crow" in the story, the crows have to run to the back of the room on their side. The seagulls chase the crows and try to tag them before they reach the back of the room. If the seagulls tag a crow, the crow becomes part of the seagulls' team. The same applies in reverse. If you say the word "seagull" in your story, then the crows try to tag the seagulls before they run to the back of the room on their side of the room.

Start with a practice round by telling a story and adding the word "seagull" or "crow".

# Are We the Same?
## Activities, Ideas & Themes:
### Specific Skills

WHY IS MY TEACHER (OR MY FRIEND) LEAVING MY SCHOOL?

**GOAL**

 Discuss the children's ideas first. Why do they think the teacher or friend is leaving the school?

Encourage the children to recognise the emotions that arise from this event, how it feels in their bodies and how to label the feelings we have when we miss people or grieve for them when they are no longer part of our lives.

Talk about feeling "blue" and discuss the new opportunities that come when things change.

**STRATEGIES**

 **IB** - Accompanied by music, play a game of walking backwards. The children start off walking backwards alone and then in pairs.

**DA** - This activity is divided into two parts.

Part One: When do I feel sad?

Facilitate conversations about grief – who has felt it before, who has lost someone (a pet, a person, a toy, a competition, a change of school, a change of address, and so on)? Invite the children to draw a picture of what it is like to feel sad.

Part Two: When do I feel happy?

Facilitate conversations about happiness arising from new experiences, such as getting a new pet, moving to a new house, being given a new toy, and expectations about new teachers and friends at a new school. Invite the children to draw pictures of what it is like to feel happy.

Movie resource for both feelings: Play the scene from "Despicable Me 2" where Gru is very sad/very happy or use scene of "Inside Out".

 **Closing Activity** - Play the song "Happy" by Pharrell Williams and have the children dance along. Use coloured paper confetti to throw on each other while dancing.

HURTING OTHER PEOPLE (2 OR 3 SESSIONS)

Note : Use Solution Organizer - Problem solving skills if required. Appendix 9

## GOAL

Bullying is not okay! Talk about bullying and boundaries, self-perception, perception of others, and resilience. Understand what constitutes bullying behaviour. Discuss productive coping strategies that foster growth and positive self-talk rather than self-defeating, negative self-talk. Talk about when to ask an adult for help.

## STRATEGIES

**IB** - Toilet Paper Mummy Game. During this game it is important to be gentle and respect each others' space.

Discuss with the children what this means.

To play this game, divide the group into teams of about four or five. Give each team a roll of toilet paper and a roll of masking tape. Each team selects a volunteer from their group. The goal of the game is to wrap the child up in toilet paper and create the best-looking 'toilet paper mummy'.

The teams have ten minutes to wrap the child up using only the toilet paper and masking tape. After ten minutes, the facilitator tells the teams to stop. Have the mummies model their awesome wrapped-up selves and ask the team members to present/"sell" their mummies, talking about why their mummy is the best.

The judge (facilitator) will have to decide which team has the best-looking mummy. The team with the best-looking mummy wins the game!

**DA** - Talk about why some people bully other people and how we can change it. Understand the reasons behind the behaviour of the bully.

Using a white board, draw pictures to help illustrate your points. In some cases, children can become bullies because they have trouble managing strong emotions like anger, frustration, or insecurity.

In other cases, children have not learned cooperative ways to work out conflicts and understand differences. There is no excuse for bullying, but it is important to understand why it happens, so that we can learn how to develop strategies to manage bullying behaviour.

**How do we solve the problem of bullying?**

Have the children think of some solutions and facilitate a discussion in which they choose the best ones. They can draw and colour the relevant pictures in their workbooks.

**RLX** - Ask the children to lie down on yoga mats or cushions for a 'becoming calm' relaxation session. Help them learn to take a deep breath, as it has a physical effect on our body to calm down and lower stress.

## HOW TO BEHAVE ON THE SCHOOL BUS.

**GOAL**

Promoting the use of safety procedures, good manners, and respect for others' space.

**STRATEGIES**

With this subject, it is very important to encourage the children to think for themselves. The facilitator pretends to be a school bus driver and outlines a situation.

The 'bus driver' explains that the children on the bus are fighting, yelling, calling each other names, kicking, opening windows, throwing things out of the windows, unlocking their seat belts, and so on.

The driver asks the children why they think this is happening and how to solve these problems. Together, the children will develop problem-solving skills, and suggest options.

The facilitator draws pictures on a large piece of paper, illustrating the children's suggestions. The drawing will stay on the wall until the next session.

PLANTS AND ANIMALS HAVE FEELINGS TOO. THEY CAN BE HAPPY AND THEY CAN BE UNHAPPY. FEEL FREE TO EXPAND THIS THEME TO BRING OTHER THEMES SUCH AS AWARENESS ABOUT WATER, THE RESOURCES ON OUR PLANET, AND HOW TO USE THEM WISELY! BE CREATIVE!

**GOAL**

Respect and awareness about other living things on the planet earth, and respect for nature.

**STRATEGIES**

**IB** - Zoo Game: A group of children chooses to stand or sit in a circle, with everyone facing the centre. Each child takes it in turn to go into the centre of the circle and represent an animal or plant.

Now everyone must choose an animal to represent themselves. Each player will have a specific animal that they represent by a hand gesture. For example, a player could put their arm up by their nose to represent an elephant or they can hold out one of their hands in a claw shape to form the paw of a lion.

Players can use their imagination for how they want to represent their animal, just as long as it's not too difficult to mimic quickly. No two players can have the same animal or have a similar hand gesture, so that no one gets confused.

Memorise each player's hand gesture and make sure everyone else knows all the animals in play. Encourage the children to choose a different animal or plant from those chosen by the other children and guess the animals.

**DA** -This activity takes place in two stages.

Stage One: When do plants and animals feel sad?

Facilitate conversations about how we can see when they are feeling this way (such as when a plant needs water or an animal is being left at home while everyone else goes out). Invite the children to draw pictures of animals and plants feeling sad.

Stage Two: When do plants and animals feel happy?

Facilitate conversations about how we can see when plants and animals are happy. Invite the children to draw pictures of animals and plants feeling happy.

Movie resource: "The Lorax", "Avatar", "A Bug's Life", "WALL–E", "Happy Feet", "Free Willy", "Chicken Run", and "Finding Nemo", are all good choices to illustrate how plants and animals have feelings.

**RLX**: Tell the story of "The Little Green Tree".

**Closing activity**: With music playing in the background, place a small leaf and a small paper fish in each child's hand.

You can also plant a tree with children in the garden and teach them how to water the tree every week.

# Are We the Same?

## Appendices

Appendix 1:

 # Children Learn What They Live

If children live with criticism,
They learn to condemn.
If children live with hostility,
They learn to fight.
If children live with ridicule,
They learn to be shy.
If children live with shame,
They learn to feel guilty.
If children live with encouragement,
They learn confidence.
If children live with tolerance,
They learn to be patient.
If children live with praise,
They learn to appreciate.
If children live with acceptance,
They learn to love.
If children live with approval,
They learn to like themselves.
If children live with honesty,
They learn truthfulness.
If children live with security,
They learn to have faith in themselves and others.
If children live with friendliness,
They learn the world is a nice place in which to live.

# Who is Responsible?

It is human nature to blame our circumstances or other people for many things.

Today, instead of complaining about something because it is not your job, or it is not working, how about asking ourselves,

"What can I do to make it better?"

# The Parable of Responsibility

This is a story about four people:

Everybody,

Somebody,

Anybody,

and Nobody.

There was an important job to do, and Everybody was asked to do it.

Everybody was sure that Somebody would do it.

Anybody would have done it, but Nobody did it.

Somebody got angry because it was Everybody's job.

Everybody thought Anybody would do it,

but Nobody realised that Anybody would not do it.

It ended up that Everybody blamed Somebody,

when Nobody did what Anybody could have done.

Unknown author of a condensed version of Charles Osgood's *A Poem About Responsibility*.

 This poem can be explored with the children. It is inspiring to encourage them to be
aware of their power to change their own choices, actions, and decisions.

# The Story of the Sun, the Moon & the Stars

How to play: Each child chooses a character and the facilitator draws the chosen symbol, a sun, a moon or a star, on the hand of each child or use stickers.

While the facilitator tells the story, each character gets up, walks around, and sits down again when their symbol is mentioned.

Gradually, the facilitator accelerates the pace of the story.

## The Sun, the Moon & the Stars

By day, the sun shines.
But in the evening, the sun goes to sleep.
And who appears when the sun goes to sleep?
The moon!
Yes! The moon and the stars appear when the sun goes to sleep.
They are all in the sky, the sun, the moon, and the stars.
Then the sun speaks to the moon, saying, "Goodnight, Moon!"
And the moon responds, "Goodnight, Sun!"
The stars also want to be wished goodnight, like the sun and the moon!
Then the sun and the moon speak together, saying "Goodnight Stars!"
And the stars, shining happily, reply, "Goodnight Sun, Goodnight Moon! See you tomorrow!"

# The Story of
# Prickles the Porcupine

## by Ithia Farah

Once upon a time, in a place named Porcupine Land, there were a lot of porcupines.

The porcupines had a problem. When it was very cold, they wanted to cuddle up together to keep warm, but when they did, they hurt each other with their quills. Quills are large, stiff hairs but they are like tiny needles with sharp tips. Their spines look like spikes.

One said, "Ow! Go away!" Another said, "Take care with your spines, you are hurting me!"

One porcupine, named "Prickles" was a very kindly porcupine. He wanted to help the others! But what could he do? He had spines as well.

Then Prickles had an idea: "I know!" he thought, "Let's move far away from each other, so that no one gets hurt!"

And so that's what they did. But although no one was getting hurt anymore, they were still cold and they had a new problem. They were so far away from each other that they had to shout to hear what the other porcupines were saying.

How could they solve their problems? How could they be close to one another without anyone getting hurt, so that they could be warm and hear what the other porcupines were saying?

Prickles thought some more, and decided that the porcupines could huddle close enough together so that they could keep each other warm, without getting so close that they were pressed together and hurting one another with their spikes.

He shouted his idea to all the other porcupines, and they tried it out. They all huddled into a group, so they could keep each other warm, but with enough space between each of them that no one was getting hurt. It worked perfectly, and no one had to shout anymore!

Prickles and all the other porcupines were then, living very happily.

**Conclusion:** We can be close to other people and still respect each other's space. It's important to listen to other people and understand that just because they want some space it doesn't mean they don't value our friendship. We can look after each other without getting so close because it's uncomfortable for everyone. Make sure we take the time to check in with other people to see how they are feeling. Do they need more space? Are they okay or do they feel we are too distant? Explore this story as a group exercise developing a role play with the children. The children can dramatise the story, using rounded chopsticks to represent the porcupine spines (but keep enough distance between the children so no one gets hurt!)Exploring personal space is fun. Talk about space invaders to develop communication and social skills!

# The Green World

by Ithia Farah

There is a very old story of a world that was all green.

Can you imagine that? Houses, clothes, trees, fruits, cars, the sky, everything; every little thing was green. All the creatures, from the ants and the worms to the elephants and the giraffes, were green.

Papa Green, Mama Green and their Baby Green children lived on the green planet. They were used to the greenness of their world and thought that everything everywhere was green, because that was all they had ever known. Until the day that a beautiful star appeared in the sky. It was gorgeous! They were amazed! It was so colourful!

The star came closer and closer to the green planet, and Papa Green, Mama Green, and all their children were terrified. They didn't know what this strange and colourful thing was, and they were scared.

"There's no need to be afraid," the star said. "I am the star of the Universe!"

"What's the Universe?" asked Papa and Mama Green.

The star thought the best way to explain would be to show them by taking them on a trip through space. So the star invited them to see some of the other planets.

Papa and Mama Green and their children climbed onto the star and travelled through space to see the other planets. It was such a surprise! They were amazed!

"What are these things?" asked Papa and Mama Green.

"Colours," explained the star, "there are many, many different colours in the universe."

After many wonderful hours, the star took Papa and Mama green and all their children back to their own planet. Now their home would be very different! They wanted to be surrounded by all the beautiful colours!

The star taught Papa and Mama Green the magic of colours. There were so many possibilities! The star showed them how to mix blue and red to make purple, yellow and red to make orange, and blue and yellow to make… green! It really was magical! The only limit was their imagination!

All the people living on the green planet saw what Papa and Mama Green had done, and they began colouring their homes and gardens too, each in his own way, choosing different colours for different things. Pretty soon the green planet had to change its name.

Now it is called the rainbow world!

# Peter & the Stars

by Ithia Farah

Peter spent all his time daydreaming. People would say to him, "Peter, you have your head in the clouds!" But Peter didn't mind, he was happy dreaming of amazing places and exciting adventures.

Peter had a good life. He had a loving family, and a very clever dog called Lucky.

Lucky was Peter's best friend and they did everything together. Lucky kept Peter company while Peter's mum was at work.

Peter liked his life, but it sometimes felt a bit boring. Every day seemed to be the same. Get up, go to school, come home, do his homework and his chores, and then go to bed. Peter wished that one of the adventures he daydreamed about would come true. Peter was so used to dreaming up new ideas that one afternoon, when he was watching his favourite film, he drifted away and found himself in the middle of the stars. He wasn't sure if it was real or if it was just another daydream!

Peter was not worried about the answer, but he was curious to know how he and Lucky could be floating in space without any space suits!

He looked at Lucky and laughed. Lucky's ears were sticking right up, because there was no gravity. He looked very funny. Lucky barked, but out in space it sounded more like a muffled 'Ruff' than the loud 'Woof' he did on Earth.

Peter asked, "What is it, Lucky?"

Lucky started flying towards a vast castle, which was floating among the stars, surrounded by fluffy white clouds. Peter was very confused, but he decided to follow Lucky.

They arrived at the castle. It was a huge building made of great big blocks of dark stone, with an immense wooden door right in the centre.

Peter felt a little bit scared, but pushed the door gently to see if it would open. To his surprise, it swung back to reveal an enormous entrance hall with a wide staircase winding upwards. The inside of the castle was lit by rainbow lights, and it made everything look very beautiful, but it was like nothing that Peter had ever seen before.

"Come on, Lucky, let's go and explore!" Peter whispered.

There was no need to ask twice! Lucky was halfway up the stairs before Peter had even stepped into the hall. Lucky wagged his tail and barked loudly, "Woof, Woof!" making the same happy noise that he did on Earth.

As Peter reached the bottom of the staircase, he saw a boy in the distance, right at the top of the stairs. He was too far away for Peter to see him clearly, but as the boy approached, Peter was scared.

"Are you... ME?" Peter stammered.

"Yes, I'm your Self," the boy replied.

"What do you mean? Why are you out there?" Peter asked, feeling very confused.

"Because you have not been listening to your Self lately, and I thought if you could see me then you might listen to me!"

Peter's 'Self' said, "Always have the courage to follow your dreams and do the things that you love. That will make a difference to your future."

They spoke for a long time, talking about the things that Peter loved, like animals and nature, until suddenly Peter's 'Self' began to float into the air. He invited Peter to fly too. It felt amazing!

Side by side they flew, until gradually they grew closer and closer, until Peter and his 'Self' were just one person again. Then Peter and Lucky began to fly back home. The stars were shining brightly, and they stopped one last time to look around and admire the beauty of the universe.

Suddenly, a voice drifted out of nowhere: "Captain! Are we ready for the expedition?"

Another voice replied, "Yes! Prepare for landing! We will be on Planet X in seconds! We need to know about new cultures and different lives. Peter will be with us! He can study the plants and animals!"

Peter saw a spaceship flying beside him. He blinked, and when he looked again he saw that the spaceship was on his TV screen, in his favourite movie. Peter stood up quickly, feeling dizzy. Was he awake or was he still dreaming?

He looked at Lucky, who was sleeping peacefully in his bed. Funnily enough, though, his ears were sticking right up, as if there was no gravity.

Peter looked down and saw that there was a book beside him on the sofa. It was all about different jobs that people do, and it was open at a page about people who work with animals, including vets, zookeepers, and police dog trainers.

Peter felt really happy! Deep in his heart, he knew that he would work with animals in the future.

Yes! He would love to look after the animals on our planet Earth.

And maybe one day, he would get to work on other planets too!

# Growing Smiles

### a Poem for Kids

A smile is quite a funny thing,
It wrinkles up your face,
And when it is gone, you never find
Its secret hiding place.

But far more wonderful it is
To see what smiles can do;
You smile at one, he smiles at you,
And so one smile makes two.

He smiles at someone since you smiled,
And then that one smiles back;
And that one smiles, until in truth
You fail in keeping track.

Now since a smile can do great good
By cheering hearts of care,
Let's smile and smile and not forget
That smiles go everywhere!

Unknown author

# Love Respects

by Paul Jensen Jr.

Love respects everyone always,
Love respects everyone's way of life,
Everyone's way of living needs respect,
Love respects everyone always :)

Love respects everyone's opinions,
Love helps us understand everyone's choices, Respecting everyone's
choices encourages understanding,
Love respects everyone's opinions :)

Love respects our needs and desires,
Love knows our needs include respect,
Our desires need respect to be understood, Love respects our needs and
desires :)

Love respects family always,
Love understands a family's influence,
Our parents' decisions need respect
Love respects family always :)

## Solution Organizer - Problem solving skills

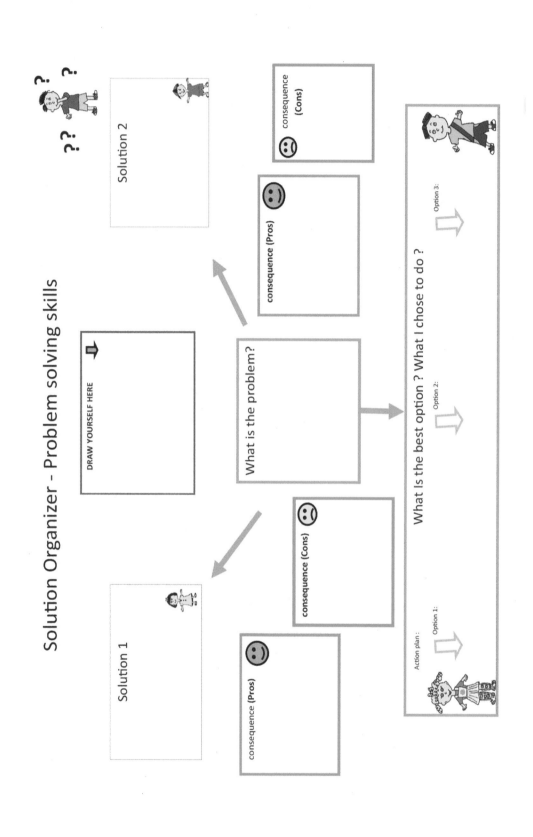

# Bibliography

Abdul-Malik I. The presuppositions of NLP. Anchor Point 1997; 11(6).

American Psychiatric Association (2013). *Diagnostic and statistical manual for mental disorders* (5th Ed). Washington.

Atherton JS. Learning and teaching. Experiential Learning [Online, UK, 2013]. Retrieved on April 16, 2015, from http://www.learningandteaching.info/learning/experience.htm

Australian childhood Foundation - Practice Guide Creating positive social climates and home-like environments in therapeutic care- Centre for Excellence in Therapeutic Care - Published: February 2019

Bear MF, Connors BW, Paradiso MA. Neuroscience: exploring the brain. Philadelphia: Lippincott

Beard CM, Wilson JP. Experiential learning: a best practice handbook for educators and trainers, 2nd ed. London / Philadelphia: Kogan Page; 2006.

Beck, JS (2011). Cognitive behavior therapy: Basics and beyond (2nd ed.), New York, NY: The Guilford Press.

*Beever S. Happy kids happy you: using NLP to bring out the best in ourselves and the children we care for paperback. Camarthen, UK: Crown House Publishing; 2009.*

*Behavior support, and transition to school. Journal of Emotional and Behavioral Disorders 10 (3): 149–57.*

Beyondblue: https://www.beyondblue.org.au/personal-best/pillar/supporting-yourself

Bilyk B. Reflective Essay: Kolb's experiential learning cycle. Norderstedt: GRIN Verlag; 2013.

Brown, Jenny - Growing yourself up: how to bring your best to all of life's relationships. Auckland: F.  le Publishing; 2012.

Can.  ⁀len; Beadle, Sally; Farrelly, Anne ;Forster, Ruth and Dr. Kylie Smith - Building resilience in children  young people - Early Childhood Development (DEECD) - University of Melbourne

Cast (2018). ⌐  ʳsal Design for Learning Guidelines version 2.2. Retrieved from http://

Center on the Deve⌐  ⌐ Child at Harvard University (2017). Three Principles to Improve Outcomes for Children and Families.  ⌐·//www.developingchild.harvard.edu (https://developingchild. harvard.edu/resources/three- ⌐ʳ-childhood-development-principles-improve-child-family-outcomes/)

Damasio A. The error of Descartes: emo⌐ʳ⌐, ʳeason and the human brain. São Paulo: Companhia das Letras; 1996.

Delucia-Waack J, Kalodner CR, Riva MT. Group cou⌐ʳʳlling and psychotherapy. Oaks: Sage Publications; 2014.

Developmental Milestones and the EYLF and NQS - https://www.dss.gov.au/our-responsibilities/families-and-children/publications-articles/developmental-milestones-and-the-eylf-and-nqs

Dilts R, DeLozier J. Map and territory (Part 2). Anchor Point 1997; 11 (6).

Early Childhood Intervention Australia Ltd (ECIA) I https://www.ecia.org.au/

Edinburgh: Heriot-Watt University; 2001.

Field C. Life skills for kids: equipping your child for the real world. New York: Random House; 2000.

Fritzen SJ. Dynamics of recreation and games. Rio de Janeiro: Vozes; 1985.

from https://trove.nla.gov.au/work/180799996?selectedversion=NBD51284116

Frost, L., & Bondy, A. (2002). The Picture Exchange Communication System Training Manual.

Gender Neutral Pronouns | LGBT Resource Center | USC. Retrieved June 17, 2020, from https://lgbtrc.usc.edu/trans/transgender/pronouns/

Goleman D. Emotional intelligence: the revolutionary theory that redefines what is to be smart Rio de Janeiro: Lens; 1995.

Graeff FG. Neuroanatomy and neurotransmitter regulation of defensive behaviors and related emotions in mammals. Braz J Med Biol Res. 1994; 27:811-29.

Griffith TL, Fuller MA, Northcraft GB. Facilitator influence in group support systems: intended and unintended effects. Information Systems Research. 1998; 9(1):20-36.

Guideline: sexual harassment - complying with the Equal Opportunity Act 2010 / Victorian Equal

Hammond W. Principles of strength-based practice. Alberta: Resiliency Initiatives; 2012.

Health across the gender spectrum- Internet Enduring Material, Sponsored by the Stanford University School of Medicine. Presented by the Department of Pediatrics at Stanford University School of Medicine. https://developingchild.harvard.edu/resources/ and https://med.stanford.edu/cme.html

James W. What's an emotion? Mind. 1994; 9:188-205.

Jeruzalinky A. Psychoanalysis and child development: an interdisciplinary approach. Porto Alegre: Artes Médicas; 1988.

*Joseph, G.E., & P.S. Strain. In press. Building positive relationships with young children. Young Exceptional Children.*

Kerns, C. , M., Renno, P., Storch, E. , A., Kendall, P. , C., & Wood, J. , J,. (2017). *Anxiety in Children and Adolescents with Autism Spectrum Disorder.* Academic Press.

Lazarus RS. Childality and adaptation. 3rd ed. Rio de Janeiro: Zahar; 1974.

LeDoux JE. The emotional brain: the mysterious foundations of emotional life. Rio de Janeiro: Lens; 1998.

Liebmann M. Art therapy for groups: a handbook of themes and exercises. New York: Rutledge;2004.

*Lise Fox,Glen Dunlap,Mary Louise Hemmeter,Gail E. Joseph,and Phillip S. Strain.The Teaching Pyramid - Model for Supporting Social Competenceand Preventing Challenging Behavior in Young Children - Bredekamp. S., & C. Copple, eds. 1997. Developmentally appropriate practice in early childhood programs. Rev. ed. Washington, DC: NAEYC. Dodge, D.T., & L. Colker. 2002. The creative curriculum. 5th ed.*

Machado ABM. Functional neuroanatomy. Rio de Janeiro: Atheneu; 1993.

Mascovici F. Interchildal development: group training. Rio de Janeiro: José Olympio; 1998.

Mascovici F. Reason emotion: emotional intelligence in question. Salvador: House of Quality; 1997.

McAtee, M., Carr, E. G., Schulte, C., & Dunlap, G. (2004). *A Contextual Assessment Inventory for Problem Behavior: Initial Development*. Journal of Positive Behavior Interventions 6 (3), 148-165.

McEvoy, P. , M., Saulsman, L. , M., & Rapee, R. , M. (2018). Imagery-Enhanced CBT for Social Anxiety Disorder. Guilford Publications

Miranda RL. Besides the emotional intelligence. London: Elsiever; 1997.

Moller C. Employeeship: how to maximize childal and organizational performance. London: Pioneer; 1996.

Mussen PH, Conger JJ, Kagan J. Child development and childality. New York: Harper and Row of Brazil; 1977.

Nolte DL, Harris R. Children learn what they live: parenting to inspire values. New York: Workman Publishing; 1998.

O'Donoghue, T., & Punch K. (2003) *Qualitative Educational Research in Action: Doing and Reflecting.* London: Routledge

Opportunity & Human Rights Commission. - Version details. (2020). Retrieved 18 February 2020,

Pfeiffer JW, Ballew AC. Using structured experiences in human resource development. Volume 1.University Associates Training Technologies Series. San Diego: University Associates; 1988.

Phelan TW. 1-2-3 Magic: effective discipline for children 2-12. Glen Ellyn:  Parentmagic; 2008.

PositivePsychology.com - Helping You Help Others. Retrieved June 30, 2020, from https:// positivepsychology.com/

Publishing, Co.(Ages & Stages Questionnaires® (ASQ-3) and (ASQ®:SE-2)

Raising Children - Stress management: https://raisingchildren.net.au/guides/first-1000-days/ looking-after-yourself/stress-grown-ups

Rapp C. The strengths model: case management with people suffering severe and persistent mental illness. New York: Oxford Press; 1988.

Richardson R. Change your thoughts, change your life with NLP. BT Elite; 2010

Shanker, D., Stuart. (2016). Self-Reg. Penguin.

Shanker, S. (2020). *Reframed*. University of Toronto Press.

Shanker, S. Help your child deal with stress - and thrive: the transformative power of self-reg. London: Yellow Kite.2018

Shanker, Stuart- Discussion Guide: Self-Reg - The MEHRIT Centre | www.self-reg.ca; 2018- Resources online and website/podcast: https://self-reg.ca/learn/parent-portal/

Shechtman, Zipora - Group Counseling and Psychotherapy with Children and Adolescents: Theory, Research and Practice. Lawrence Erlbaum Associates Inc 2006

Squires, J., Bricker, D. D., & Twombly, E. (2015). Asq-Se-2 users guide. Baltimore: Paul H. Brookes

Steiner, C. (2003). Emotional literacy. Fawnskin, Calif.: Personhood Press.

Stress and stress management: grown-ups. The Australian Parenting Website https:// raisingchildren.net.au/

Supporting yourself- https://www.beyondblue.org.au/personal-best/pillar/supporting-yourself

The Early Years Learning Framework (EYLF) - (COAG) on 2 July 2009.

The Equal Opportunity Act 2010 - Victorian Equal Opporunity. Retrieved January 27, 2020, from https://www.humanrightscommission.vic.gov.au/the-law/equal-opportunity-act

The Special Educational Needs and Disability Act. About Learning Disabilities. In: McCashen M. The strengths approach. Victoria: St. Luke's Innovative Resources; 2008.

The Special Educational Needs and Disability Act. Brief Guidelines for Lecturers and Teachers.

The Stressed Detective - Self-Reg with Dr. Stuart Shanker: https://self-reg.ca/stressed-detective

The UDL Guidelines. Retrieved June 30, 2020, from http://udlguidelines.cast.org/

Three Early Childhood Development Principles to Improve Child . Retrieved June 17, 2020, from https://developingchild.harvard.edu/resources/three-early-childhood-development-principles-improve-child-family-outcomes/

Three Principles to Improve Outcomes for Children and Families. Retrieved June 24, 2020, from https://46y5eh11fhgw3ve3ytpwxt9r-wpengine.netdna-ssl.com/wp-content/uploads/2017/10/ HCDC_3PrinciplesPolicyPractice.pdf

Walsh, B. E. (2011).Vak self-audit: visual, auditory, and kinesthetic communication and learning styles: exploring patterns of how you interact and learn. Victoria, BC: Walsh Seminars Pub.House

What is Be You? https://www.youtube.com/watch?v=gnA8v_HUJDQ

Williams & Wilkins; 2001.

Winnicott DW. Playing and reality. Tavistock Publications; 1971

# About the Author

Ithia Farah- Assoc. MAPS - BSc (Psych) Hons - Clinical and Educational Licentiate Degree in Psychology - Brazil – Associate Member of the Australian Psychological Society (APS).

Ithia thrives on change and innovation, and she is a passionate professional who loves to work with children and their families.

Ithia has extensive experience in the clinical and educational fields and has been developing and delivering evidence-based practices such as early intervention programs, social skills groups, emotional regulation and behaviour management plans for children and their families for 25 years. In Brazil, she worked as a clinical psychologist and was a co-founder of the NGO "Carpe Diem" to support children and young people with disability. Since 2007 in Australia, she has worked in the Early Childhood Intervention sector in non-profit organisations.

Ithia's debut publication *Are We The Same?* - Children's Activity Colouring Book received the National Foundation for Educational Development Award (1999) and sold 46,000 copies. The book was sponsored by the Ministry of Education and Culture (MEC-Brazil) with an official stamp award from the government. *Are We The Same* was distributed to all public schools in 27 states across Brazil and was implemented in the school curriculum to be used by the National Foundation of Educational Development (FNDE). It is a national project to support the full participation and inclusion of all children within all settings, with educational and therapeutic workshops to promote capacity building to teachers and parents on how to best use the activity book with children, in mainstream schools or at home.

**For more information on the Are We The Same? project and the author:**

**ECIA /NSW - Please see article on:**
http://blog.eciansw.org.au/2017/03/are-we-the-same/
**Facebook:** www.facebook.com/childrenbookarewethesame
**Linkedin:** http://www.linkedin.com/in/ithiafarah

Associate Member
Australian
Psychological
Society Assoc MAPS